EMBRACING THE UNCERTAIN
LEADER GUIDE

Embracing the Uncertain
A Bible Study for Unsteady Times

Embracing the Uncertain
978-1-7910-4089-5
978-1-7910-4090-1 *eBook*

Embracing the Uncertain: Leader Guide
978-1-7910-4097-0
978-1-7910-4098-7 *eBook*

Embracing the Uncertain: DVD
978-1-7910-4099-4

Also from Magrey R. deVega:

Awaiting the Already:
An Advent Journey Through the Gospels

One Faithful Promise:
The Wesleyan Covenant for Renewal

Hope for Hard Times:
Lessons on Faith from Elijah and Elisha

Savior:
What the Bible Says about the Cross

The Bible Year:
A Journey through Scripture in 365 Days

Questions Jesus Asked:
A Six-Week Study in the Gospels

LEADER GUIDE

Magrey R. deVega

EMBRACING THE UNCERTAIN

A Bible Study for Unsteady Times

Abingdon Press | Nashville

EMBRACING THE UNCERTAIN
A Bible Study for Unsteady Times
Leader Guide

Copyright © 2025 Abingdon Press
All rights reserved.

No part of this work may be reproduced or transmitted in any form or by any means, electronic or mechanical, including photocopying and recording, or by any information storage or retrieval system, except as may be expressly permitted by the 1976 Copyright Act, the 1998 Digital Millennium Copyright Act, or in writing from the publisher. Requests for permission can be addressed to Rights and Permissions, The United Methodist Publishing House, 810 12th Avenue South, Nashville, TN 37203-4704 or emailed to permissions@abingdonpress.com.

978-1-7910-4097-0

Scripture quotations unless otherwise noted are taken from the Common English Bible, copyright 2011. Used by permission. All rights reserved.

Scripture quotations marked NRSVue are taken from the New Revised Standard Version, Updated Edition. Copyright © 2021 National Council of Churches of Christ in the United States of America. Used by permission. All rights reserved worldwide.

Book cover for *Embracing the Uncertain: A Bible Study for Unsteady Times, Leader Guide* by Magrey R. deVega. The image shows a large tree with leaves in four seasonal colors—green, yellow, orange, and dark red—blending together. Leaves and birds drift away into a cloudy sky.

MANUFACTURED IN THE UNITED STATES OF AMERICA

CONTENTS

INTRODUCTION 7

SESSION 1: The Desperate Father and the Uncertainty of Faith 11

SESSION 2: Peter and the Uncertainty of Forgiveness 21

SESSION 3: The Crowd and the Uncertainty of Worry 29

SESSION 4: Lazarus and the Uncertainty of Mortality 39

SESSION 5: Zacchaeus and the Uncertainty of Surrender 47

SESSION 6: Jesus and the Uncertainty of Obedience 55

INTRODUCTION

In *Embracing the Uncertain,* Magrey deVega offers biblically based suggestions for how to keep moving through the uncertain, unsettled, and unstable times of our lives. Such times may come about for any number of reasons: political unrest, economic difficulties, family conflict, or personal struggle. Through all of these trials, we can learn to be more like Christ—not trying to push through everything with sheer force of will nor shrinking in fear and waiting for it all to pass without effort on our part. Rather, Christ moved through many uncertainties with composure and assurance by walking with God through it all.

This leader guide is intended to help you lead a small group of adults from your congregation in a study of *Embracing the Uncertain* in order to learn biblical approaches for getting through trying times. This guide provides logistical pointers, Scripture readings, and study questions you can use to plan and lead six sessions, corresponding to the six chapters of *Embracing the Uncertain*:

Session 1: The Desperate Father and the Uncertainty of Faith

This week focuses the story of Jesus healing the boy with the unclean or impure spirit at the request of his father in Mark 9:14-29.

It explores the complex interplay and intertwining of doubt and belief in our lives, encouraging readers to bring their doubts into the open.

Session 2: Peter and the Uncertainty of Forgiveness

This session centers on Matthew 18:21-35, which includes some of Jesus's teaching on forgiveness. It explores the nature of forgiveness and its relationship to God's kingdom and our calling to help build that kingdom.

Session 3: The Crowd and the Uncertainty of Worry

This session discusses Luke 12:1-34, which contains an array of disparate teachings from Jesus. The focus of the session is the theme of worry and our propensity to forget, ignore, or otherwise feel bereft of God's presence in difficult times. We are called to constantly remember God's presence and provision in order that we may draw on this comfort when God might seem distant.

Session 4: Lazarus and the Uncertainty of Mortality

John 11:1-44 recounts one of the most well-known of Jesus's healing miracles, in which he brings Lazarus back from the dead. This story provides a rich jumping-off point for thinking theologically about death, resurrection, embodiment, and what really matters in this life.

Session 5: Zacchaeus and the Uncertainty of Surrender

The session this week examines Luke 19:1-10, the story of Zacchaeus. This brief but rich story involves themes of our seeking and knowing God and Christ, God and Christ seeking and knowing us, the nature of grace, and how material possessions and wealth fit into the life of faith.

Session 6: Jesus and the Uncertainty of Obedience

The key passage for this session, Matthew 26:36-46, is a scene from the garden of Gethsemane near the end of Jesus's life. This provides a point of departure for reflecting on our calling to follow and obey God and Christ even as they lead us beyond where we may have expected or even wanted to go. This session also includes some discussion questions on the bonus chapter, which concerns the different narratives of Christ's resurrection in the Gospels.

Each session plan in this leader guide contains the following:

- **Session Goals** help you focus on the outcomes most relevant and helpful to your group.
- **Biblical Foundations** are the main Scripture texts in each session, printed from the Common English Bible without verse numbers and section headings to support reading each passage as a whole unit. The participant guide notes verses where they are relevant to the discussion.
- **Before Your Session** includes basic preparation tips.
- **Starting Your Session** contains ideas for "icebreaker" conversations and/or activities to prepare those in the session to actively participate in discussions and activities.
- **Discussion Questions** provide suggestions for discussion topics for your group. You will likely not have time to use all the questions provided. Choose and use them to guide and shape a lively, constructive discussion.
- **Opening and Closing Prayers** offer participants a chance to include new comments or substitute their own prayers or good wishes.

Thank you for leading your group in this study! May you find this leader guide informative and helpful as you facilitate your group's deeper engagement with the Bible and what it has to teach us about navigating life's uncertainties.

SESSION 1
THE DESPERATE FATHER AND THE UNCERTAINTY OF FAITH

Session Goals

This session's readings, discussion, and reflection will help participants:

- More deeply consider the nature of doubt and how it figures into a life of faith.
- Understand that faith and doubt are often intertwined, that doubts are an unavoidable and healthy part of faith.
- Think more clearly and compassionately about their own doubts, both theological and otherwise.
- Be more able to reconcile doubts and questions with a life of deep faith.

Biblical Foundations

Someone from the crowd responded, "Teacher, I brought my son to you, since he has a spirit that doesn't allow him to speak. Wherever it overpowers him, it throws him into a fit. He foams at the mouth, grinds his teeth, and stiffens up. So I spoke to your disciples to see if they could throw it out, but they couldn't."

Jesus answered them, "You faithless generation, how long will I be with you? How long will I put up with you? Bring him to me."

They brought him. When the spirit saw Jesus, it immediately threw the boy into a fit. He fell on the ground and rolled around, foaming at the mouth. Jesus asked his father, "How long has this been going on?"

He said, "Since he was a child. It has often thrown him into a fire or into water trying to kill him. If you can do anything, help us! Show us compassion!"

Jesus said to him, "'If you can do anything'? All things are possible for the one who has faith."

At that the boy's father cried out, "I have faith; help my lack of faith!"

Noticing that the crowd had surged together, Jesus spoke harshly to the unclean spirit, "Mute and deaf spirit, I command you to come out of him and never enter him again." After screaming and shaking the boy horribly, the spirit came out. The boy seemed to be dead; in fact, several people said that he had died. But Jesus took his hand, lifted him up, and he arose.

Mark 9:17-27

So, brothers and sisters, because of God's mercies, I encourage you to present your bodies as a living sacrifice that is holy and pleasing to God. This is your appropriate *priestly service. Don't be conformed to the patterns of this world, but be transformed by the renewing of your minds so that you can figure out what God's will is—what is good and pleasing and mature.*

Romans 12:1-2

Before Your Session

- Carefully read and reread this session's Biblical Foundations. Note words and phrases—especially repeated words and phrases—that attract your attention, and think about what they might mean to you and to others in your group. Write down your questions and try to answer them. You may want to consult trusted Bible commentaries.
- Carefully read the introduction and chapter 1 of *Embracing the Uncertain*. Note topics about which you want to know more; you may want to consult reputable sources for further information.
- You will need: Bibles for in-person participants and/or slides with Scripture texts (identify the translation); newsprint or markerboard and markers (for in-person sessions); paper, pens or pencils (in-person).
- If using the DVD or streaming video, preview session 1. Choose the best time in your session plan for viewing.

Starting Your Session

Make sure that participants know that what others share during sessions shouldn't be shared with others outside of class since, especially with the topics of uncertainty and doubt, honesty and vulnerability can be essential in the process of learning and growth. We don't want these sessions to add more uncertainty! Participants should feel free to share without judgment or fear.

Ask participants to name things that they have uncertainty about—things that involve aspects of the unknown or unknowable. The list can be varied, involving matters that are personal, political, environmental, related to the church, or anything else. Depending on group size and other factors, consider writing down the responses on newsprint or a whiteboard to keep track of them. Ask participants the following:

- Do you also have or have you had uncertainty about these areas of your life?
- What are some strategies that you have found helpful here? What has helped you reduce fear and anxiety, increase assurance, or otherwise get you through uncertain times?
- Specifically, how has God or your Christian practice helped you?
- Are there any ways in which you think your Christian beliefs or practices have made these uncertainties more complex or difficult?

Opening Prayer

Lord God, we pray that our time together in these sessions will build us up to weather the storms of fear, doubt, and uncertainty in all of our lives. We ask you to grant us the faith, clarity, and wisdom to be able to learn to live through these trying times, admit our doubts, and draw ever closer to you on our journey. Amen.

Watch the Session 1 Video

Discuss:

- What statements in this video most interested, intrigued, surprised, or confused you? Why?
- What questions does this video raise for you?

Healing the Boy

Discuss:

- The man in the story from Mark 9 approached Jesus's disciples sure that his son would be healed. "But," as Magrey writes, "as often happens when one chooses to follow Jesus, the man did not get what he was hoping for. The ending did not meet his expectations. *His boy was still as sick as ever, and he was starting to lose faith*" (emphasis added). Have you ever had a similar experience, where your faith didn't lead you to what you expected or even desired? What happened?
- When Jesus learns about the situation and that the disciples were unable to help, he says, "You faithless generation, how long will I be with you? How long will I put up with you?" (Mark 9:19). Why does Jesus respond this way? How do you understand his words here?
- Magrey notes that the disciples "were having trouble believing Jesus when he *was* around, imagine what it would be like when he wasn't." How do you see the disciples in the Gospels? They often don't seem to understand Jesus's teachings in the narrative. Why do you

think that is? What changes between the Gospels and Acts of the Apostles for them?
- Have you or a loved one ever experienced something akin to the dark emotional or mental state of the young boy in Mark 9:14-29? What kind of support and resources are helpful amid such a crisis?

However and Therefore

As Magrey notes in the text, a key moment comes in Mark 9:24: "Immediately the father of the child cried out, 'I believe; help my unbelief!'" (Mark 9:24 NRSVue). This statement is somewhat peculiar in that it seems to be saying two things at once—that he believes and also needs God's help due to not believing. Perhaps we can fill in the missing step that links these two ideas. Adding "however" or "therefore" between these statements connects them in slightly different ways, each suggesting an interpretation of the father's words.

Discuss:

- After the man's exclamation in Mark 9:24, Jesus does not respond verbally at all, saying nothing to the man. How do you understand this? Why does Jesus not say anything?
- Magrey first suggests linking them with "however": "Yes, we believe. However, we still doubt." Sometimes we have secure beliefs that are shaken by events in our lives or the world or things we learn in school or elsewhere. Have you ever had moments like this? What events in your life or ideas you have encountered have shaken the framework of your beliefs or your ideas about God?

- After such events or ideas came into your life, how did you reconcile them with your beliefs? Was this a process of acceptance? Growth? Strengthening? How would you describe it?
- Magrey notes that adding "therefore" suggests "that belief and unbelief go together. Because belief exists, unbelief exists as well. I believe; therefore, help the unbelief that naturally comes with it. In other words, certainty and uncertainty... are necessary co-companions in your journey of life." How do you understand this idea? How is it different from what you get by linking the father's statements with "however"? Have you found this to be the case in your own experience?
- "Faith is not the absence of doubt, but the embrace of it and ultimately the transformation of it." Do you agree with Magrey's statement here? How do you see the relationship between faith and doubt? How have you engaged with doubt on your faith journey?
- According to Magrey, the addition of "therefore" offers us an important lesson: "Don't settle for easy answers in life. Don't ever stop the thirst for learning, for checking your assumptions, for embracing the unknown. Don't ever stop maturing in your faith. Admit your doubts and acknowledge your questions." How has your faith matured over the years? What does the process of becoming more mature in faith mean to you? How has your understanding of the meaning of Christian faith changed or shifted over the years?
- Were you raised as a Christian and did you accept this identity, or was it something that you came to later in life?

Either growing up or in the process of becoming Christian, how did you experience the relationship between doubt and belief?
- Has the nature of your doubts and questioning changed over time? If so, how?

Faith and Doubt

Discuss:

- Magrey writes that one of Thomas Merton's books "conveys an intimacy with God when God seems most distant.... It is the fusion of these extremes, in creative tension, that has contributed" to the power of his writing for many. Can you think of any examples, whether in the Bible, your own life, or in people of faith throughout history, where distance from God has led to a kind of enrichment of faith or spiritual life? What are some potential positive sides to these moments of distance?
- Read the first words of Thomas Merton's prayer again: "My Lord God, I have no idea where I am going. I do not see the road ahead of me. I cannot know for certain where it will end. Nor do I really know myself, and the fact that I think I am following your will does not mean that I am actually doing so."[1] Which parts of this do you find helpful? Does the knowledge that even a formidable writer and teacher like Merton felt doubt bring comfort to you? How?
- Merton's prayer goes on to say that he isn't sure if he is following God's will even if he thinks he is in the moment. What role does God's will play in your life? How do you

try to discern God's desires for you and your life? How do you determine whether you are on the right path? Can you truly know you are following God's will?
- Merton suggests that the desire to do God's will is pleasing to God in itself, and sometimes that is all we have to hold on to. What do you make of this idea? Do you think this is a good way to understand God and your relationship to God? What might be helpful about this idea?
- Where is there uncertainty in your life, especially in your faith? What would it mean to embrace that uncertainty? How might doing so lead you to deeper faith?

Call to Action

Either during the session time or on your own during the week, spend some time writing a prayer in your own words that expresses both your doubts and your confidence in God. You may find it helpful to write out the specific nature of your doubts that in some way connect to the concerns of the father in Mark 9. What are you most anxious about? What do you have both faith and doubt about? Where in your life do you find yourself saying, "I believe; help my unbelief."

Closing Prayer

God, thank you for grounding me with confidence and guiding me through doubt. I will strive to embrace my doubts, knowing that they are part of faith and that you offer your compassion and steadfastness to all who doubt. I pray that I may learn how best to follow you, always grateful for your grace and forgiveness when I falter and fall short. I believe; help my unbelief. Amen.

---

1. The text of the prayer can be found online at https://onbeing.org/blog/thomas-mertons-prayer-that-anyone-can-pray/

SESSION 2
PETER AND THE UNCERTAINTY OF FORGIVENESS

Session Goals

This session's readings, discussion, and reflection will help participants:

- Consider Jesus's teaching on forgiveness in Matthew.
- Think theologically and deeply about the meaning of forgiveness and its place in our lives.
- Come to a deeper understanding of and appreciation for God's forgiveness.
- Appreciate how practicing forgiveness helps build up God's kingdom.

Biblical Foundations

Then Peter said to Jesus, "Lord, how many times should I forgive my brother or sister who sins against me? Should I forgive as many as seven times?"

Jesus said, "Not just seven times, but rather as many as seventy-seven times."

Matthew 18:21-22

When Joseph's brothers realized that their father was now dead, they said, "What if Joseph bears a grudge against us, and wants to pay us back seriously for all of the terrible things we did to him?" So they approached Joseph and said, "Your father gave orders before he died, telling us, 'This is what you should say to Joseph. "Please, forgive your brothers' sins and misdeeds, for they did terrible things to you. Now, please forgive the sins of the servants of your father's God."'" Joseph wept when they spoke to him.

His brothers wept too, fell down in front of him, and said, "We're here as your slaves."

But Joseph said to them, "Don't be afraid. Am I God? You planned something bad for me, but God produced something good from it, in order to save the lives of many people, just as he's doing today. Now, don't be afraid. I will take care of you and your children." So he put them at ease and spoke reassuringly to them.

Thus Joseph lived in Egypt, he and his father's household.

Genesis 50:15-22

Therefore I say to you, whatever you pray and ask for, believe that you will receive it, and it will be so for you. And whenever you stand up to pray, if you have something against anyone, forgive so that your Father in heaven may forgive you your wrongdoings.

Mark 11:24-25

Before Your Session

- Carefully read and reread this session's Biblical Foundations. Note words and phrases—especially repeated words and phrases—that attract your attention, and think about what they might mean to you, and to others in your group. Write down your questions and try to answer them. You may want to consult trusted Bible commentaries.
- Carefully read chapter 2 of *Embracing the Uncertain*. Note topics about which you want to know more; you may want to consult reputable sources for further information.
- You will need: Bibles for in-person participants and/or slides with Scripture texts (identify the translation); newsprint or markerboard and markers (for in-person sessions); paper, pens or pencils (in-person).
- If using the DVD or streaming video, preview session 2. Choose the best time in your session plan for viewing.

Starting Your Session

Forgiveness is a central theme in the Bible and is also a key part of Christian faith.

Offer the prompts and questions below to your group. This may be done as a guided meditation, in which you ask the questions and participants are given time to think through their answers silently. Depending on group dynamics and the level of comfort in the group, you may also offer these questions for open discussion after participants have been given time to consider their responses.

- Think about a time you were forgiven for something. It could be something small or large, something important or trivial, something from your childhood or from yesterday.
- Think about what you did and how you felt about it at the time. What were your thoughts and emotions?
- What, if any, difference did forgiveness make for you? What was the experience of forgiveness like?
- Think about a time you have forgiven someone for something.
- How did you come to forgive them? Was it difficult? Easy? Did you regret forgiving or waiting to forgive?
- How did this act of forgiveness change you? Did it change how you felt about this person or what they had done? How did this affect your relationship with them?

Opening Prayer

Merciful God, be with us and guide us today as we open our hearts to you, to each other, and to the world as we consider the place of forgiveness in our lives. Grant us the compassion, understanding, and humility of our Savior Jesus Christ as we move through this world, knowing that often we must empower ourselves to forgive just as surely as we have been forgiven by you. Amen.

Watch the Session 2 Video

Discuss:

- What statements in this video most interested, intrigued, surprised, or confused you? Why?
- What questions does this video raise for you?

Forgiveness

Discuss:

- Magrey notes that Peter asked Jesus how many times to forgive because he was self-seeking and was looking for a compliment. Do you understand the passage and Peter's question this way?
- Do you ever feel uncertain when it comes to forgiveness? Do you question whether you should or even can forgive in some cases? What do you do in these circumstances, when it is difficult to know how to move forward? Do you have any spiritual practices or questions you ask yourself when difficult situations arise about forgiveness?
- Think about times in your life when it was difficult to forgive a wrong that had been done to you. What made forgiveness hard?
- Think about the times when you have caused harm to someone else. Have you fully sought forgiveness for whatever you did? What would help in repairing your relationship with that person?
- Mostly, when we talk about forgiveness, we are talking about it on the interpersonal level, from one individual to another—just as you might forgive your friend or parent or coworker for something they did to you (or vice-versa). But does anything change when we think of forgiveness as a kingdom-building action on a broader social or even societal level?

- What difference does it make for you to see the act of forgiveness as not just a private act between two people but as participation in God's grand act of restoring all of broken creation?
- Magrey relates a story from another pastor about going to the home of a couple and finding that one of them had harbored resentment for a long time. Have you ever seen a similar situation, one in which yourself or another felt unable to forgive over a long period and thus damaged the relationship? What happened? What actions, resources, and practices can you think of that might help people move toward genuine forgiveness?
- Consider the definition of forgiveness offered by Magrey: "Forgiveness means owning your attitudes and your actions and saying to the other person, 'I choose not to hurt you anymore, regardless of what we have done to each other in the past.' Then, forgiveness means you make the conscious choice to decentralize the impact of that hurt in your life." Is this different from how you usually understand forgiveness? In what ways? What are some other possible ways of conceiving of forgiveness?
- For many, the cross is a symbol of forgiveness. As Magrey says, "There you'll find the greatest model for forgiveness humanity has ever received. And thank God for it because it is in God's forgiveness of us that we discover true freedom and true healing." How do you understand the relationship between the cross and forgiveness, and what role does this play in your faith?

- Magrey is clear that forgiveness is not the same as forgetting; it is not about just wiping the slate clean as soon as possible. However, he writes, "We are called to forgive, nonetheless.... In the end, we must believe that forgiveness is not optional in the Christian life." Practically, what do you think this means? Are there any limits to this calling? Are we called as Christians to forgive *anything* another does to us or others?
- Where is there uncertainty in the act of granting forgiveness? Where is there uncertainty in asking for or receiving forgiveness? How can you work to embrace the uncertainty in forgiveness, and what would that mean?
- Think about ways in which you might be called to forgive yourself. What would be required for you to experience the grace and mercy of God, move past your guilt and shame, and claim the life of peace that God wants for you?

Call to Action

During this week, spend some time in prayer asking God to help you recalibrate your motivation for forgiveness. Begin by thanking God for all the ways you have been forgiven throughout your life. Meditate on the ways that such acts of forgiveness have shaped your life positively and have helped in building up the kingdom of God on earth. You may want to bring up and meditate on local or global stories you have heard that describe the power of forgiveness and think about how these stories fit with God's work of restoring a broken world. Ask God for help in joining this work and consider ways you can improve your practice of forgiveness toward yourself and others.

Closing Prayer

Gracious God, thank you for forgiving me of my sins. Empower me to follow the example you set for us in Jesus, that I might both forgive others and seek forgiveness. Guide me to discern the appropriate times and places to forgive. Help me to participate in the work of your kingdom, spreading forgiveness and reconciliation for all. Amen.

SESSION 3
THE CROWD AND THE UNCERTAINTY OF WORRY

Session Goals

This session's readings, discussion, and reflection will help participants:

- Sort out the multiple themes circulating throughout Jesus's teaching in Luke 12.
- Consider what following God means in terms of what kind of life it leads to and the ways in which difficulty and suffering might still be part of that life.
- Come to a more keen appreciation of the ways in which God is working in our lives in the present moment.

Biblical Foundation

Jesus said to them, "Watch out! Guard yourself against all kinds of greed. After all, one's life isn't determined by one's possessions, even when someone is very wealthy." Then he told them a parable: "A certain rich man's land produced a bountiful crop. He said to himself, What will I do? I have no place to store my harvest! Then he thought, Here's what I'll do. I'll tear down my barns and build bigger ones. That's where I'll store all my grain and goods. I'll say to myself, You have stored up plenty of goods, enough for several years. Take it easy! Eat, drink, and enjoy yourself. But God said to him, 'Fool, tonight you will die. Now who will get the things you have prepared for yourself?' This is the way it will be for those who hoard things for themselves and aren't rich toward God."

Luke 12:15-21

Then Jesus said to his disciples, "Therefore, I say to you, don't worry about your life, what you will eat, or about your body, what you will wear. There is more to life than food and more to the body than clothing. Consider the ravens: they neither plant nor harvest, they have no silo or barn, yet God feeds them. You are worth so much more than birds! Who among you by worrying can add a single moment to your life? If you can't do such a small thing, why worry about the rest? Notice how the lilies grow. They don't wear themselves out with work, and they don't spin cloth. But I say to you that even Solomon in all his splendor wasn't dressed like one of these. If God dresses grass in the field so beautifully, even though it's alive today and tomorrow it's thrown into the furnace, how much more will God do for you, you people of weak faith! Don't chase after what you will eat and what you will drink. Stop worrying. All the nations of the world long for these things. Your Father knows that you need them. Instead, desire his kingdom and these things will be given to you as well."

Luke 12:22-31

Now, it is commendable if, because of one's understanding of God, someone should endure pain through suffering unjustly. But what praise comes from enduring patiently when you have sinned and are beaten for it? But if you endure steadfastly when you've done good and suffer for it, this is commendable before God.

You were called to this kind of endurance, because Christ suffered on your behalf. He left you an example so that you might follow in his footsteps. He committed no sin, nor did he ever speak in ways meant to deceive. When he was insulted, he did not reply with insults. When he suffered, he did not threaten revenge. Instead, he entrusted himself to the one who judges justly.

1 Peter 2:19-23

Before Your Session

- Carefully read and reread this session's Biblical Foundations. Note words and phrases—especially repeated words and phrases—that attract your attention, and think about what they might mean to you and to others in your group. Write down your questions and try to answer them. You may want to consult trusted Bible commentaries.
- Carefully read chapter 3 of *Embracing the Uncertain*. Note topics about which you want to know more; you may want to consult reputable sources for further information.
- You will need: Bibles for in-person participants and/or slides with Scripture texts (identify the translation); newsprint or markerboard and markers (for in-person sessions); paper, pens or pencils (in-person).

- If using the DVD or streaming video, preview session 3. Choose the best time in your session plan for viewing.

Starting Your Session

Ask participants: What things do you worry about in your life now? Briefly discuss some of the responses.

Next, read the following prayer to the group out loud or choose a volunteer to do so:

God grant me the serenity to accept the things I cannot change,
Courage to change the things I can,
and the Wisdom to know the difference.

This is most widely known as the Serenity Prayer and is perhaps most famous through its association with Alcoholics Anonymous. There are quite a number of versions, so people may be familiar with it with slightly different wording, sometimes with additional lines. There is no authoritative "original" version of the prayer, though the idea seems to have originated in the early 1930s with the one of the preeminent Protestant theologians of the era, Reinhold Niebuhr. He invoked some version of it in public speeches, and it slowly spread through newspapers and word-of-mouth in various Christian groups.

Ask participants:

- Have you heard this prayer before? What do you think of it? (Clarify that this is absolutely not a request for people to disclose their involvement in Alcoholics Anonymous or similar groups.)
- How many of the things mentioned as what worries us can actually be changed?

- What times in your life have you had to accept things that you realized you could not change? What happened?
- Have there been times in your life when you also had a realization that something you had previously accepted or resigned yourself to actually could be changed?
- What tools are available or how have you tried to cultivate the wisdom to know the difference between what we must accept and things we need to change?

Opening Prayer

Ever-present God, we pray to you today knowing that you are here with us, in our midst, watching over us and guiding us. We know that you will always be with us, and we pray that we may have the insight and understanding to know that you are beside us in every moment of our lives. Amen.

Watch the Session 3 Video

Discuss:

- What statements in this video most interested, intrigued, surprised, or confused you? Why?
- What questions does this video raise for you?

Worry and Uncertainty

Discuss:

- Magrey points out the sheer variety of themes touched on in Luke 12: criticism of the Pharisees, warnings about the world, the futility of chasing earthly possessions, the need for vigilance about judgment, Jesus's own calling to bring division, and words of comfort about God's care for birds and lilies. How might these themes be connected? What ties them together?

- Considering the whole of Luke 12, Magrey writes, "We see that the comfort of God does not transport us away from the darkness of this world but actually drills us more deeply into the midst of it. To consider ourselves as lilies and ravens does not mean that God will make life easier for us, for that may not be the case." What are some examples in history or in your own life that a life of faith in God does not mean a more comfortable existence? In what ways can faith improve one's life? How might God's care be seen as helping us in distinct ways?
- Some strains of Christianity have been criticized as glorifying suffering, in part because if we consider Christ as our exemplar of faith and his suffering and death as for our salvation, then we may see our own suffering in a positive light. How does the notion of suffering, either your own or in general, figure into your faith? How do you think God sees human suffering in different circumstances?
- Look at the Serenity Prayer in the Starting Your Session section of this chapter. How does this prayer connect to Jesus's command in the Scriptures not to worry? Do you see them as effectively saying the same thing, or are there some meaningful differences?
- Consider the parable of the rich man in Luke 12. What examples in your life have you seen of the kind of thinking the man in the parable exhibits, storing up a wealth of resources for a future that might not come?

What teaching do you think Jesus was trying to get across in this parable? How do you or might you follow this teaching in your own life?
- More generally, how do you understand the role of material possessions and wealth in light of your faith? How does faith shift your perspective on material possessions and how they should be counted, stored, and used?
- What is the difference between peace and comfort? How can we experience peace that surpasses understanding even in the absence of comfort?
- Has there ever been a time when you worried about something a great deal, only to have it work out to be better than you feared? What contributed to bringing about a better resolution than you thought?

God's Presence and Provision

- Magrey points out that when Jesus is talking about God's comfort and care for us, "he actually offers a challenge: to see the condition of the world in such a way that we can notice the presence, activity, and provision of God in the midst of it." What practices, thoughts, or actions help you see the presence and provision of God in your life? What do you think is most helpful for increasing our sense of God's presence?
- As Magrey notes, a sense of God's presence is perhaps most important and most difficult to maintain when we are in our toughest moments. Have you ever felt abandoned by God, perhaps like Jesus on the cross, when he cried, "My

God, my God, why have you forsaken me?" (Matthew 27:46 NRSVue). (Note that this is a reference to Psalm 22:1, which is a psalm of complaint and lament but ultimately focuses on thanking and praising God for deliverance.) Was there anything that changed your thinking for the better in these moments?

- In our difficult moments, God is surely present, but as Magrey notes, God's work may not be revealed until later. Have you experienced this in your own life or can you think of other examples of it? Have there been times when God was at work, though this could not be seen at the time but was only understood later?
- Think about what Magrey says about adults and children and the differences in their "attentional spotlight." Have you ever had instances when a child or someone else unexpectedly noticed something important that others missed? What happened?
- Notice also the related quotation from Alison Gopnik, which includes the statement, "Children explore, adults exploit." How might these ideas relate to Jesus's saying in Matthew 18:3 (NRSVue), "Truly I tell you, unless you change and become like children, you will never enter the kingdom of heaven"? What is Jesus trying to communicate here? What characteristics of how children think or act does Jesus think might be important for those who follow him?

Call to Action

During this week, take some time to reflect in a journal about the many ways that God has provided for you throughout your life, without your seeing or acknowledging it at the time. These don't have to be miraculous or grand examples. Think about even the tiniest blessings that you know you could not have achieved on your own or merited by your own achievement. Consider this list to be your "Lily and Raven" list, which you can refer back to (and add to) when you go through episodes of worry, reminding you of God's presence and provision.

Closing Prayer

God, I thank you that just as your eye is on the sparrow, your watchful, caring gaze is always upon me, protecting and providing for me each day. Grant to me the ability to see in the middle of my difficulties, that I might not be so fixated on my troubles, but observant of your unfailing grace and love. Amen.

SESSION 4
LAZARUS AND THE UNCERTAINTY OF MORTALITY

Session Goals

This session's readings, discussion, and reflection will help participants:

- Understand and interpret the story of Lazarus in John 11.
- Think more deeply about Christian understandings of death, mortality, resurrection, afterlife, and the body.
- Consider how we can prepare today for the life that awaits us after death.

Biblical Foundations

When Jesus arrived, he found that Lazarus had already been in the tomb for four days. Bethany was a little less than two miles from Jerusalem. Many Jews had come to comfort Martha and Mary after their brother's death. When Martha heard that Jesus was coming, she went to meet him, while

Mary remained in the house. Martha said to Jesus, "Lord, if you had been here, my brother wouldn't have died. Even now I know that whatever you ask God, God will give you."

Jesus told her, "Your brother will rise again."...

When Mary arrived where Jesus was and saw him, she fell at his feet and said, "Lord, if you had been here, my brother wouldn't have died."

When Jesus saw her crying and the Jews who had come with her crying also, he was deeply disturbed and troubled. He asked, "Where have you laid him?"

They replied, "Lord, come and see."

Jesus began to cry. The Jews said, "See how much he loved him!" But some of them said, "He healed the eyes of the man born blind. Couldn't he have kept Lazarus from dying?"

Jesus was deeply disturbed again when he came to the tomb. It was a cave, and a stone covered the entrance. Jesus said, "Remove the stone."

Martha, the sister of the dead man, said, "Lord, the smell will be awful! He's been dead four days."

Jesus replied, "Didn't I tell you that if you believe, you will see God's glory?" So they removed the stone. Jesus looked up and said, "Father, thank you for hearing me. I know you always hear me. I say this for the benefit of the crowd standing here so that they will believe that you sent me." Having said this, Jesus shouted with a loud voice, "Lazarus, come out!" The dead man came out, his feet bound and his hands tied, and his face covered with a cloth. Jesus said to them, "Untie him and let him go."

John 11:17-23, 32-44

Our citizenship is in heaven. We look forward to a savior that comes from there—the Lord Jesus Christ. He will transform our humble bodies so that they are like his glorious body, by the power that also makes him able to subject all things to himself.
Philippians 3:20-21

Before Your Session

- Carefully read and reread this session's Biblical Foundations. Note words and phrases—especially repeated words and phrases—that attract your attention, and think about what they might mean to you, and to others in your group. Write down your questions and try to answer them. You may want to consult trusted Bible commentaries.
- Carefully read chapter 4 of *Embracing the Uncertain*. Note topics about which you want to know more; you may want to consult reputable sources for further information.
- You will need: Bibles for in-person participants and/or slides with Scripture texts (identify the translation); newsprint or markerboard and markers (for in-person sessions); paper, pens or pencils (in-person).
- If using the DVD or streaming video, preview session 4. Choose the best time in your session plan for viewing.

Starting Your Session

Toward the beginning of the chapter, Magrey reflects on his role as a pastor at funerals and memorial services he has helped plan and preside over, noting the power of the stories people tell about someone who has passed. He writes, "Getting the stories started is fairly easy. But then the storytelling takes on a life of its own. The stories come randomly, from different members of the family, with no predetermined order or flow.... In one moment, a family member will tell a riot of a tale that sends everyone into stitches, and then in the blink of an eye, that family member will catch a breath and become weepy."

Discuss:

- Have you ever had an experience like this?
- Have you found funeral or memorial services or similar ceremonies and gatherings to be helpful in the process of memorializing and grieving?
- Have you ever attended a funeral or memorial service (or come across information with some other means) and learned something about the deceased person that you didn't know, or were you given the chance to see that person in a different light?
- What moments that had an impact on you can you recall from funeral services or when you were with someone near death?

Opening Prayer

God, you are the Lord of our life and death. We thank you for the lives we have been given and the bodies we have been granted to experience this world of wonder and beauty. And we pray that we may face the end of our lives with comfort, peace, and the assurance that, as in life, in death we will never be without your loving presence. Amen.

Watch the Session 4 Video

Discuss:

- What statements in this video most interested, intrigued, surprised, or confused you? Why?
- What questions does this video raise for you?

Making Order from Chaos

Discuss:

- How has your attitude toward death shifted over time? Has it changed with age? Health concerns? With the development of your faith?
- Have there been times in your life when you were preoccupied with or worried about your own mortality? What was happening in your life that caused this? Is there anything in particular that gave you the strength to wrestle through this? Did you come to any conclusions during this process?
- In what ways can you identify with Mary and Martha in the story? What profound and difficult questions have you ever asked of God in the wake of a loved one's death?
- Magrey writes that "the power of the Resurrection and the promise of new life are not simply things that await us when we die, but they can also inform our hope and even our behavior in the way we live today. It's right here with us. He is right here with us." How does this understanding influence how you live now? What does it change in your actions, ways of thinking, or ways of seeing the world?

- Have you found it to be true that people are most remembered for their human relationships after they die? Do you think about your own death and your legacy on earth? How do you want to be remembered after your death?

Resurrection and the Body

Discuss:

- As Magrey notes, the Bible offers a wide variety of ideas about the afterlife, with perhaps none being definitive and providing an unmistakably clear picture. What different ideas about the afterlife, both ones you found far-fetched and plausible, have you encountered?
- Numerous passages in the Bible speak of a bodily resurrection. Has this idea figured into your thoughts about the afterlife before? How so? Do you believe this is an essential part of Christian faith? Is it possible to exist in some sense without a body?
- What questions do you have about what things will be like after we die? What do you wonder about?
- Think about Paul's use of the seed and the plant as a metaphor for our resurrected bodies. As Magrey summarizes, "We then sprout up into new life, with a new kind of body that is heavenly, not earthly, but still very much uniquely us and still a body in some way. Your heavenly or spiritual body will be uniquely and individually yours, with the same essence, the same life, as your earthly body." Is this idea helpful to you? What insight does it provide, if any?
- Because our bodies will be redeemed and resurrected, resurrection is something that, in some meaningful sense,

we can begin to experience in this life. Jesus, likewise, speaks of the Kingdom as both a future and a present reality, as both here and not yet. What can you do today to experience a new life, a foretaste of the Resurrection?

Call to Action

Make a two-column list with the headings "I Believe" and "I Don't Know." During the week, under each heading, write down both your firm ideas about death and the afterlife as well as the things you do not understand sufficiently or have open questions about. Try to be specific, but remember that there may be overlap between the two columns; there can be things you firmly believe that you also have questions and a lack of understanding about.

Over several days, pray over your lists, thanking God for what you are able to see through faith and also the gift of mystery that reminds us that God is greater than our comprehension. Look over the list from time to time and pay attention to how the Holy Spirit may be guiding you to embrace the uncertain.

If time permits, you may ask participants at the end of the session to share some of the things they would put on each side of their lists. This may help others in brainstorming and getting started.

Closing Prayer

God, thank you for sending Jesus, who is the resurrection and the life. Teach me to trust in you, as Christ did at every moment, even unto death. I pray for faith and trust, especially when I am grieving and troubled. Though I do not understand everything now, and I know that my questions will remain with me all my days on this earth, grant me the secure knowledge of eternity with you. Amen.

SESSION 5
ZACCHAEUS AND THE UNCERTAINTY OF SURRENDER

Session Goals

This session's readings, discussion, and reflection will help participants:

- Consider the story of Zacchaeus and what it can tell us about seeking, finding, and understanding God and Christ.
- Come to a greater appreciation of the ways in which God seeks out each of us, drawing us into relationship with God.
- Think about the concepts of freedom and material possession in a Christian theological context.

Biblical Foundations

Jesus entered Jericho and was passing through town. A man there named Zacchaeus, a ruler among tax collectors, was rich. He was trying to see who Jesus was, but, being a short man, he couldn't because of the crowd. So he ran ahead and climbed up a sycamore tree so he could see Jesus, who was about to pass that way. When Jesus came to that spot, he looked up and said, "Zacchaeus, come down at once. I must stay in your home today." So Zacchaeus came down at once, happy to welcome Jesus.

Everyone who saw this grumbled, saying, "He has gone to be the guest of a sinner."

Zacchaeus stopped and said to the Lord, "Look, Lord, I give half of my possessions to the poor. And if I have cheated anyone, I repay them four times as much."

Jesus said to him, "Today, salvation has come to this household because he too is a son of Abraham. The Human One came to seek and save the lost."

Luke 19:1-10

In Christ I have a righteousness that is not my own and that does not come from the Law but rather from the faithfulness of Christ. It is the righteousness of God that is based on faith. The righteousness that I have comes from knowing Christ, the power of his resurrection, and the participation in his sufferings. It includes being conformed to his death so that I may perhaps reach the goal of the resurrection of the dead.

It's not that I have already reached this goal or have already been perfected, but I pursue it, so that I may grab hold of it because Christ grabbed hold of me for just this purpose.

Philippians 3:9b-12

Before Your Session

- Carefully read and reread this session's Biblical Foundations. Note words and phrases—especially repeated words and phrases—that attract your attention, and think about what they might mean to you, and to others in your

group. Write down your questions and try to answer them. You may want to consult trusted Bible commentaries.
- Carefully read chapter 5 of *Embracing the Uncertain*. Note topics about which you want to know more; you may want to consult reputable sources for further information.
- You will need: Bibles for in-person participants and/or slides with Scripture texts (identify the translation); newsprint or markerboard and markers (for in-person sessions); paper, pens or pencils (in-person).
- If using the DVD or streaming video, preview session 5. Choose the best time in your session plan for viewing.

Starting Your Session

One of the distinctive aspects of Christian belief emphasized by Methodists is John Wesley's concept of prevenient grace. Magrey defines it in the following way: "It is the grace that goes before us, before we are even able to recognize it or understand it, which has been at work in our lives since the moment we were born. It is never static, always on the move, always luring us, wooing us, searching for us, and drawing near to us. In other words, in the fashion of Luke's Gospel, it is the grace of God that is constantly *passing through* our lives."

Another way of explaining this idea starts with the fact that nobody comes to Christ, God, and the gospel totally on their own. There's always a history there, a set of circumstances, a path that was laid out by God. This might include constellations of events, family members, friends, pastors, personal choices, books, memories—anything that has led you to God.

Ask participants to reflect on this idea in their own lives. Discuss:

- Have you come across this idea of prevenient grace before? Where? If you didn't have a sense of this idea before then, how did it change your theological understanding?
- Think about your own faith journey or times when you came closer to God. Looking back, how do you see God's prevenient grace at work in your life? How did God prepare the way for you?

Opening Prayer

God, we long for you. We seek you out, wanting to know you. Sometimes, we find you easily; we feel you in our hearts as sure as we feel our own breath. Other times, your presence seems far from us, and we find ourselves feeling utterly lost, without your love. We pray that we may stand close beside you, knowing that your presence never truly leaves us and that even before we knew you, you had prepared the way for us to find you. Amen.

Watch the Session 5 Video

Discuss:

- What statements in this video most interested, intrigued, surprised, or confused you? Why?
- What questions does this video raise for you?

Making Order from Chaos

Discuss:

- Did you ever feel a desire to know Jesus, like Zacchaeus? Maybe you had already been in the church or had read the

Gospels but suddenly found a desire to get closer to him and understand him and his teachings?
- Have you found in your time learning about Jesus that you discovered different sides of or aspects to Jesus? Have you or do you now go through periods where you understand him, his work, and his identity in different ways? For example, we can see Jesus as a personal savior, friend, and companion; the one who frees us from sin; a rebel who pushed against the powers that be; a spiritual revolutionary; a religious reformer; a complicated man with a unique relationship to God; and as Godself on earth. All of these are possible ways of seeing and understanding Jesus, just with different emphases and points of view.
- Commenting on Philippians 3:10-11, Magrey writes, "Maybe Paul, just like the blind man and Zacchaeus, actually gives us permission to acknowledge the uncertainty and tentativeness we feel when it comes to knowing and following Jesus." What uncertainties do you feel about knowing Jesus? What things do you feel you want to know about Jesus or would be helpful to you in some way?
- If Jesus were to call you down from a tree and invite himself over for a meal with you, what kinds of conversation topics would you want to cover? What changes in your life do you think Jesus would ask of you?
- Do you feel or think that God is seeking you, searching for you, and looking at you right now? How do you know? What does this mean in your life?

- Do you feel known by Jesus? If so, how? What does that mean to you?
- Consider Paul's desire to want to know Christ and the power of his resurrection. In what ways are you longing to experience the Resurrection today? How might you pray that God might reveal that power to you? What are you willing to give up so that you can experience that power?
- Magrey writes, "God has been searching for you, watching you, long before you realized it. That realization leads to such a transformation." How has the idea of God searching for you affected your faith? Your understanding of God and your relationship to God?

Freedom and Wealth

- Quoting Anthony Bloom, Magrey discusses the "freedom that comes from surrendering one's full life over to God"—a freedom that is built on love rather than material wealth. What is this freedom that we receive when we turn to God? What do we give up, and what do we gain? How might it be different from worldly freedom or common political understandings of freedom?
- Part of the Zacchaeus story deals with the role of our material possessions and wealth. How do you understand the connection between material things and freedom or the lack of it? More generally, how do wealth and possessions fit into your faith and what you feel called to by Jesus?

Call to Action

Spend some moments in silence every day over the upcoming week. Target at least fifteen minutes, or whatever is most feasible for you. During that silence, find a centering word or phrase that you can use to refocus your silence whenever your mind starts to drift. You might choose a word or phrase from this story of Zacchaeus or the words of Paul, such as "I want to see Jesus," or "I want to know Christ," or "I want to welcome Jesus." Meditate on the ways in which you have known Jesus as well as how you feel Jesus and God have known you and prepared you to know them. Consider the changes in your life that Jesus may be calling you to make.

Closing Prayer

God, thank you for seeking me out, even as I have longed to see you. Lead me into a deeper experience of the death and resurrection of Jesus. Help me see their manifold meanings for us, their importance for our lives today, and their significance for our hopes about the future and our life to come. Lord, help me so that I might know your power and live the life you wish for me to live. Amen.

SESSION 6
JESUS AND THE UNCERTAINTY OF OBEDIENCE

Session Goals

This session's readings, discussion, and reflection will help participants:

- Consider the meaning and implications of obedience to God.
- Formulate strategies and practices that allow them to discern God's will and learn to follow it in their lives.
- Appreciate the importance and the effects of the Resurrection in the Christian life.
- Think about the Resurrection accounts in the Gospels and consider the distinctive emphases of each Gospel writer.

Biblical Foundations

Then Jesus went with his disciples to a place called Gethsemane. He said to the disciples, "Stay here while I go and pray over there." When he took Peter and Zebedee's two sons, he began to feel sad and anxious. Then he said to them, "I'm very sad. It's as if I'm dying. Stay here and keep alert with me." Then he went a short distance farther and fell on his face and prayed, "My Father, if it's possible, take this cup of suffering away from me. However—not what I want but what you want."

He came back to the disciples and found them sleeping. He said to Peter, "Couldn't you stay alert one hour with me? Stay alert and pray so that you won't give in to temptation. The spirit is eager, but the flesh is weak." A second time he went away and prayed, "My Father, if it's not possible that this cup be taken away unless I drink it, then let it be what you want."

Again he came and found them sleeping. Their eyes were heavy with sleep. But he left them and again went and prayed the same words for the third time. Then he came to his disciples and said to them, "Will you sleep and rest all night? Look, the time has come for the Human One to be betrayed into the hands of sinners. Get up. Let's go. Look, here comes my betrayer."

Matthew 26:36-46

When the Sabbath was over, Mary Magdalene, Mary the mother of James, and Salome bought spices so that they could go and anoint Jesus' dead body. Very early on the first day of the week, just after sunrise, they came to the tomb. They were saying to each other, "Who's going to roll the stone away from the entrance for us?" When they looked up, they saw that the stone had been rolled away. (And it was a very large stone!) Going into the tomb, they saw a young man in a white robe seated on the right side; and they were startled. But he said to them, "Don't be alarmed! You are looking for Jesus of Nazareth, who was crucified. He has been raised. He isn't here. Look, here's the place where they laid him. Go, tell his disciples, especially Peter, that he is going ahead of

*you into Galilee. You will see him there, just as he told you."
Overcome with terror and dread, they fled from the tomb.
They said nothing to anyone, because they were afraid.*
Mark 16:1-8

Before Your Session

- Carefully read and reread this session's Biblical Foundations. Note words and phrases—especially repeated words and phrases—that attract your attention, and think about what they might mean to you, and to others in your group. Write down your questions and try to answer them. You may want to consult trusted Bible commentaries.
- Carefully read chapter 6 and the bonus chapter of *Embracing the Uncertain*. Note topics about which you want to know more; you may want to consult reputable sources for further information.
- You will need: Bibles for in-person participants and/or slides with Scripture texts (identify the translation); newsprint or markerboard and markers (for in-person sessions); paper, pens or pencils (in-person).
- If using the DVD or streaming video, preview session 6. Choose the best time in your session plan for viewing.

Starting Your Session

In the Bible, people hear God in many ways. Sometimes, God speaks directly to them, even appearing before them in some kind of physical form. Others encounter God in dreams or visions. There are divine messengers and angels who speak for God. God also acts and speaks through other people and events. A theme that runs through many books in the Bible is that God is always present and is able to speak through anyone and anything.

Many if not most Christians don't experience such dramatic and clear instances of God speaking to them—if God speaks to us, it is rarely in a booming voice from the sky! Nevertheless, God is still speaking to us in many ways, though they can be subtle, and different people may have widely disparate experiences of hearing God. Discuss:

- How and when does God speak to you? This could be through other people, Scripture, a small voice you can feel, or just a sort of general sense of some kind of message.
- Have you experienced periods of divine silence? Does it seem that this was more God not speaking or you not being able to hear or aspects of both?
- How do you discern God's voice in the world? How do you know it is God?
- Have you ever heard or internally felt a literal voice or experienced what seemed to be God communicating with you directly in some way? What do you think about accounts of this kind of experience both in the Bible and more generally?
- What are different ways that you have learned to more effectively listen to God? Through study? Silence? Meditation? Conversation?

Opening Prayer

Lord God, we know that from the beginning of Creation, you have never stopped speaking to us. We pray that we may have ears to hear you, to understand your good news for us. And for those who feel cut off from your presence, for those who cannot hear your voice, we pray that they may never stop seeking after you—just as surely as we know you will always call them and prepare their way to you. Amen.

Watch the Session 6 Video

Discuss:

- What statements in this video most interested, intrigued, surprised, or confused you? Why?
- What questions does this video raise for you?

Obedience

Discuss:

- What does the idea of obedience to God mean to you? Is this part of your faith and your thinking about God? How do you discern and follow God's desires for you?
- Jesus says, "All who want to save their lives will lose them. But all who lose their lives because of me will find them" (Matthew 16:25). What does this teaching mean to you? Does it play a role in how you live out your faith?
- Consider the connection between the Scripture for this session and the Annunciation. Who are the people who have influenced you during formative times of your life, and whose impact continues to shape the choices that you make today? How might you acknowledge them, even thank them personally, or at least give thanks to God for them?
- How do you see the disciples' failure to remain with Jesus toward the end of the Gospel narratives? Was this just an expected reaction? A terrible betrayal? A justifiable attempt at self-preservation? A mix of these and more?

- What do you think the failure of the disciples in these moments is meant to teach us about our relationship to Jesus?
- Magrey asks whether we are ready for Jesus "to lead us into the difficult, uncertain places of surrender, self-sacrifice, and obedience." Do you feel ready for this? What do you think this might mean for us today? Where are these "difficult, uncertain places" that lie outside of our comfort zone that our obedience to God and Christ might lead us?
- Magrey offers that obedience to God "requires regular spiritual discipline, centered on the practice of hearing God's voice, and learning to surrender and trust." How do you or could you build this kind of discipline? What practices can or do you implement into your life that help you to hear God and act on what God is telling you?
- In the section on SOS in our spiritual lives, Magrey suggests beginning a practice of daily Scripture reading. How often do you read the Bible? Has this shifted over time or at different points in your life? Do you find reading the Bible to be a valuable spiritual practice? In what ways?
- "Prayer sometimes means talking and listening to God even though you are not sure if anyone is listening or speaking on the other end." Does Magrey's statement here resonate with you? Do you sometimes feel unsure that your prayers are being heard? How do you react to this?
- Silence has long been associated with spiritual practices and religious life, particularly as a means to quiet the mind, reduce distractions, and listen for God. Does silence play a role in your life and faith today? Do you

intentionally seek out silence? If so, how, and what do you do in these silent moments?

Resurrection

Discuss:

- Magrey, along with many others, holds that the Resurrection is the culmination of each Gospel narrative and is "the one true, reliable source for certainty in the Christian faith." What do you think of this idea? Does the Resurrection play such a role in your own thinking? What does the Resurrection mean to you?
- Do you have doubts about Christ's resurrection? Are you or have you been unsure about it in some ways or some of the details of the event? How have you dealt with doubts about this?
- What do you think of the idea that "without the Resurrection, there would be no Christianity"? What would have happened to the disciples and the gospel without the Resurrection?
- The Gospel writers specifically point out that the first people to look for Jesus after his death were not the disciples but various groups of women. What is the significance of this? What does it say about discipleship, loyalty, and our expectations, for example?
- Magrey picks up on a frequent theme of Christian theology: the redemption of all things through Christ. He writes, "The power of the Resurrection through Christ is nothing less than the power to redeem the haunting

guilt and shame of our yesterdays, the ongoing sufferings and despair of today, and the anxieties and worries of tomorrow." What does this mean, that all things will be redeemed? That we don't feel the sting of these things? That their nature is changed? That we are changed?
- At the end of the epilogue, Magrey offers summaries of how each Gospel writer is responding to uncertainties about the Resurrection and God's role in it. How do you process and understand the differences between the Gospel narratives and their resulting distinctive messages? Why do you think we have four Gospels, each with their own narratives and emphases? Why might they all be included in the Bible?

Call to Action

If time permits, at the end of the session, engage in a discussion about participants' experiences in these sessions. This can also be done individually during the week. Discuss or consider:

- What is the most surprising or interesting thing you learned or figured out during our sessions? Have you seen any aspects of your faith or stories in the Bible in a new light?
- Think back to the first session, when we listed our uncertainties. And think about uncertainties that have come up in the course of our readings and discussions. What uncertainties are you trying to embrace now? What would this mean in your life if you could embrace them?

Closing Prayer

God of power and mercy, thank you for calling me to obedience. Though I always seek you and try to do your will, forgive me for not always hearing your voice. Accept my desire to hear you as itself an offering of obedience. Lead me to a place of surrender, that I might learn how to better serve you in the world and thus also experience the joy of the Resurrection in Jesus. Amen.

Watch videos based on
EMBRACING THE UNCERTAIN
with Magrey R. deVega through Amplify Media.

Amplify Media is a multimedia platform that delivers high-quality, searchable content with an emphasis on Wesleyan perspectives for churchwide, group, or individual use on any device at any time. In a world of sometimes overwhelming choices, Amplify gives church leaders and congregants media capabilities that are contemporary, relevant, effective and, most important, affordable and sustainable.

With *Amplify Media* church leaders can:

- Provide a reliable source of Christian content through a Wesleyan lens for teaching, training, and inspiration in a customizable library
- Deliver their own preaching and worship content in a way the congregation knows and appreciates
- Build the church's capacity to innovate with engaging content and accessible technology
- Equip the congregation to better understand the Bible and its application
- Deepen discipleship beyond the church walls

Ask your group leader or pastor about Amplify Media and sign up today at www.AmplifyMedia.com.